New Orleans For Free

Paul Oswell

This guide was written by Paul Oswell and is published through Amazon by Shandy Pockets publishing (www.shandypockets.com). Follow us on Twitter (@shandypockets) and find us on Facebook if you're into that sort of thing. All material is copyright Paul Oswell, 2014.

"Champagne tastes and shandy pockets."

CONTENTS

1. INTRODUCTION
2. FREE ADVICE
3. FREE LOCAL RESOURCES
4. FREE MUSIC AND DANCE
5. FREE EATS AND DRINKS
6. MARDI GRAS
7. FREE FESTIVALS
8. FREE TOURS
9. FREE MUSEUMS
10. FREE ART AND CULTURE
11. FREE LAUGHS
12. FREE OUTDOORS
13. FREE MISCELLANY
14. YOU ARE NOW FREE TO GO

1. INTRODUCTION

As you'll soon see, this isn't a fancy guidebook filled with glossy photos and colorful maps. It's a more basic collection of information but I figure if you're travelling, you'll already have the maps and the phone apps and we just want to point you in the direction of Free Stuff.

I make no apologies for this. I want this guide to be like a local talking to you in a bar or on the street – they wouldn't start getting out photos of the places they're recommending, so neither am I. I'll send you on your way – you're clever enough to work out the rest.

I thought about calling this book The Big Free-sy, but then I realised it's an awful pun and in any case, the people that live here kind of hate that 'Big Easy' nickname. I do like awful puns, though. For the uninitiated, NOLA is by far your best bet if you're going down that civic familiarity/nickname road.

I've tried to keep inclusions in the guide as free as possible, but with some things you may need to dig out a dollar or two – buying a drink to listen to some wonderful free music in a bar or take advantage of complimentary red beans and rice. You're still getting something for free, so I figure it wasn't too big a deal. *Laissez les bons temps roulez.* Let the good times roll. You'll hear that a lot, and you'd do well to adhere to it.

I canvassed a suitably diverse cross-section of knowledgeable residents for free words of advice, and I've quoted them wherever appropriate. Here's one to get you started:

"New Orleans is not so much a Third-World American city as it is a First-World Caribbean capital."

It's a good point. New Orleans' flaws – from the potholes in the road to the relaxed attitude to urgency – are what make it so special, though. It's not a Disney-fied, picture-perfect wonderland where everything is clean and runs on time. It's one of the few American cities left with real, palpable character. You won't find global chain stores in the French Quarter, but you will probably find a place that leaves you with a story to tell, one way or the other. Embrace it.

I've included an 'Honourable Mentions' sections at the end of each chapter. While these additions are not necessarily free in the strictest sense, these are things that still represent outstanding value for money, and which almost all locals will recommend you do. It's the 25¢ Martini you can get with lunch, or the un-miss-able happy hour pizza offer. It's a little additional information, just in case you're interested. The locals call it '*lagniappe*'.

The sections are self-explanatory, so it just leaves me to leave you with some sage local advice to set you on your way:

"*People live here. We are welcoming and gracious and we want you to enjoy yourself. Explore this treasure, but respect it and us. We are the ones that maintain the magic and beauty that you're here to experience. Find a true New Orleans. The pulse and grit and sweaty rhythm. It's why you're here and not in Las Vegas.*"

Let's take a look at that Las Vegas comparison for a moment. Compared to New Orleans, Vegas touts its hedonism loudly – "Come and do shots as you throw a seven at the craps table and walk off into the night, pockets bulging with banknotes, legions of exotic strangers vying to be invited back to your hotel room," it says, waving at you while wearing a weird shiny suit and gesturing suggestively with matchplay casino chips.

But in Vegas, the fast living involves every choice being to some extent choreographed, tightly controlled and charged to your room at buttock-clenchingly high prices. The experience – as exhilarating as it may be in parts – is a generic one. It's a prescribed Las Vegas Experience, queue on the right to buy tickets and yes, that'll be 19 dollars for your frozen margarita, don't touch anything and thanks for playing.

If Las Vegas is a theme park of indulgence, New Orleans is more like a national park, where hedonism can be seen in its natural habitat, gratification is allowed to develop organically, extravagance enjoys a healthy conservation programme and eccentricity is not an endangered species. You know…Free Range Hedonism.

Welcome to enjoyment's National Park.

Thanks for the local knowledge:

Vee Anne Russ, Sarah Celino, Benjamin Black Perley, Marielle Songy, Taylor Lyon, Kyle Ruggieri, Matt Brown, Brian Bonhagen, Jade Patton, Sarah Burkitt, Leah Sarris, Victoria Lehew, @lipwrap, Judy Regan,

Jian Bastille, Larissa Cupp, Brett Axelroth, Justine Roig, Zachary Bartlett, Jacob Germain, Richard Read, Shadow Angelina, Deborah Burst, Julie Perez, Rex Dingler, Christopher Marlowe, Hal Koran, Melanie M Kuehl, TJ Bogan, Jillian Rosandich, Kira Chung, Jeanie NOLA, Seale Paterson, Bug Brockway, Jean Queen, Pope Matt Thomas.

2. FREE ADVICE

Having asked around for the single most valuable piece of advice from those that were born and raised here, I'll tell you this much. As a visitor to New Orleans, you can do one simple thing that will keep the locals from thinking less of you. It's arguably more helpful than tipping generously, praising the Saints to the high heavens or buying a big round of daiquiris.

It's simply this:

Don't call it "*N'awlins*".

No-one actually from here has ever called it that in the history of the city, apart from, perhaps, to ridicule a misguided tourist. It's a media-constructed fallacy that ranks alongside the mistruths that the locals throw 'gumbo parties' and that thousands of young girls show off their breasts to get Mardi Gras beads every year. Stay here for any substantial length of time and you'll discover that none of this actually happens.

Asking around, as I did, I was offered lots of other advice, some of which might help you out and which I here present to you here without comment. This is real, useful, local advice. You're welcome:

"Tempting as it is, don't wear Mardi Gras beads out of season. It really marks you out as a tourist."

"There are plenty of people in the French Quarter who will try and work age-old scams. The 'I know where you got 'dem shoes' one is a classic (they're on - insert street name/your feet - stupid!). Laugh and politely refuse to play."

"Don't wander into unfamiliar neighbourhoods drunk. You're a walking target, and an easy one. That seven dollar cab ride home late at night is always worth it. Keep your wits about you. Walk with purpose."

"Really, really try not to pee in public. It's one thing that the cops will pick you up on. Drink in the streets, stay up all night, be as boisterous as you like, but please pee indoors, preferably in a room that contains plumbing."

"Explore more than just the French Quarter. There's history and adventure all over the city."

"If someone offers you a free baseball cap, it's probably too good to be true."

"Don't walk with your cell phone out unless you want to get a new one. Also, it's not okay to walk alone and drunk late at night, no matter how much your significant other pissed you off."

"Buy local, tip everyone, avoid Bourbon Street."

"Either come to Nola with absolutely no plans and get weird with it or come with a very thought out idea of what you want (e.g. explore restaurants or art galleries). Too often I see tourists who are drunk and confused about what kind of experience they want."

"Bring good shoes. You'll need them if you're foolish enough to stand in line for beignets at Cafe du Monde on a Saturday morning. Supplemental note: try Morning Call at City Park."

"When attempting to figure out what a good spot for locals is, think one step ahead. If you ask a concierge, bartender, tour guide or cabby, you will get the same answer as all other tourists. This will result in you hanging out with other tourists, in a place that caters to tourists. Instead, ask questions like "How do locals find out who's playing in the area?" Investigating your environs should be more than word of mouth, especially from someone who may be on the take."

"Always be polite and respectful to the people you meet. Ask questions, but don't be too intrusive unless the person invites you to ask more about their personal life, that includes Katrina."

"Be extra polite to the people serving you food and drink. Don't ask for them to 'make it strong' because trust me, most local bars are already making it pretty strong, and ask for a double if you want to be on your ass immediately. And please educate yourself somewhat on local cuisine. No, I cannot make your seafood gumbo without seafood. Yes, Cajun and creole food tend to be spicy. No, I cannot control the amount of spice put in while cooking something that has to stew, simmer, be pre-baked/cooked or marinated unless you're at my house and I'm the one doing the cooking."

"WWOZ Livewire, Nola Defender, Humid Beings, Arts New Orleans, The Gambit, Where Y'at: these are all great resources and are your friends. These friends have special powers that can transport you to worlds only imagined."

That should give you some food for thought to be going on with.

Oh, and, by the way, it's pronounced 'NooOR-linz'.

One final thing: unless they bring it up in conversation and you feel a connection to a person, they likely don't want to talk about their Katrina experiences. The city is more than a collection of people who went through a tragedy. Watch the Spike Lee documentary 'When The Levees Broke' or, if that's too harrowing, the first season of the HBO show 'Treme'.

The city is moving on and there's SO MUCH to look forward to. And the good news? A lot of it won't cost you a cent.

3. FREE LOCAL RESOURCES

The best local listings magazines can be picked up for free in most bars, coffee shops and cafes, and have a substantial amount of actual interesting features and interviews as well as music, culture and entertainment listings. The ones to watch out for, and which between them should cover almost everything you could want to do in the city, are:

The Gambit

Probably the most established and best read of the market. Locals like to bemoan its mainstream status but it's still the most comprehensive free weekly listings paper in the city, and prints every Tuesday. (www.bestofneworleans.com)

Offbeat

A monthly glossy magazine that focuses on the local music scene. Their music listings are very good, and the interviews with local musicians are top notch. It's especially useful come festival season. (www.offbeat.com)

Where Y'at?

A full-colour, monthly newspaper that is somewhere between Gambit and Offbeat. Culture, arts and a strong eating and drinking section make it worth browsing. (www.whereyat.com)

Ambush

A monthly magazine aimed at the LGBT community. It can be picked up in most of the gay bars on Bourbon Street and in the French Quarter. (www.ambushmag.com)

Antigravity

Excellent free monthly 'alternative' newspaper, looking at more fringe and niche arts and cultural issues in the city. (www.antigravitymagazine.com)

Websites

www.nola.com (website of the Times-Picayune newspaper)

www.noladefender.com

www.humidcity.com

www.wwoz.com

Tourist Offices

Visit New Orleans

Get your free street maps and advice on local attractions and tours. 600 Decatur Street, 504 569 1482, www.visitneworleans.com

The main Convention and Visitor's Bureau has a fully-stocked help desk with leaflets for just about everything you could ever want to do in NOLA. They're in the Lower Garden District, just on St Charles Avenue, so you can easily take the streetcar. 2020 St Charles Avenue, 504 566 5011, www.neworleanscvb.com

Libraries

A message from a resident librarian: *"THE LIBRARY IS FREE. No, seriously, free wifi and computer usage at all New Orleans public libraries for everyone, even if you don't have an New Orleans Public Library card."* So there you go. Find your nearest branch at www.neworleanspubliclibrary.com

4. FREE MUSIC AND DANCE

As befits the birthplace of jazz – arguably America's most important cultural export – it's not really a matter of going out and finding free music. The city happily provides its own soundtrack, and in most of the tourist-heavy neighbourhoods, you'll find yourself serenaded from all angles. Rogue brass bands, banjo-plucking gutter punks, lone trumpeters and roaming second line parades all contribute to the near-constant musical background of any walk around downtown New Orleans.

For much of the day, Royal Street cuts a musical swathe through the historic French Quarter, with buskers of all styles and genres lining the largely-pedestrianised road. A couple of the larger, more organised outfits regularly pitch up outside Rouse's grocery store on the corner of Royal and St Peter, and a little further down just past Royal and St Louis. Towards the outer edges of the Quarter, though, you'll find clarinet players and trombonists, or ragged accordion and banjo players who look like they've been living in a train car for weeks, and most likely have been.

There's an embarrassment of riches as far as incidental music to your day goes, and it really can add an uplifting atmosphere to things as mundane as a stroll to get milk from the corner store. They're playing for tips, of course, so if you stop to take in the music for a while, be a sport and throw into the hat. Same goes for taking photos. Let's be polite, people. You don't get this level of free street entertainment in Cleveland – hell, you don't get it in New York City. Appreciate.

With this huge ocean of musical talent in the city, it's no surprise that a huge number of venues across town have musicians playing for free just to get you through the door. You'll likely have to purchase a drink to stay and watch, but the diversity and professionalism of the free entertainment on offer is astounding. The list of free music in town would fill a whole book in its own right, but here are some of the best spots to catch high quality acts without paying a cover charge.

Irvin Mayfield's Jazz Playhouse

One of the city's favourite sons hosts some truly great jazz musicians in this swanky lounge in the Royal Sonesta Hotel. Unless it's a very special guest, the early shows are free to the public – which means turning up in good time if you want to bag a seat. The place is regularly voted in the top jazz clubs in town, and though you'll have to buy a cocktail (don't worry, the bar is excellent), you still get to see some genuinely impressive performers. See the website or call for dates and times. (300 Bourbon Street, 504-553-2299, www.sonesta.com)

Jeremy Davenport Lounge

Another superb jazz trumpeter commands the luxurious space in the Ritz-Carlton Hotel every weekend. You can catch guest musicians on Wednesday evenings, but Thursdays (5.30pm-9pm), Fridays and Saturdays (9pm-1am) are when you'll hear the talented and suave Mr Davenport lead his band through the great American songbook. Again, you'll need to buy a drink, but there are free nibbles and the show is a great on (921 Canal Street, 504-524-1331, www.ritzcarlton.com).

The Spotted Cat

This little shack of a place half way up Frenchmen Street is usually brimming with people keen to see some energetic live jazz, swing and blues. There are three to four shows a day, with (usually) 2pm, 4pm, 6pm and 10pm slots. There's no cover, though the door people will let you know about the one drink minimum. Expect a lively crowd, and the venue is a special favourite of the local swing dancing community, so you'll likely get a free dance show to boot – see also **Free Dance Lessons**, below (623 Frenchmen Street, 504-943-3887, www.spottedcatmusicclub.com).

The Maison

Even though it sits squarely on Frenchmen Street, the home of the city's best known jazz clubs, there's a distinct diversity of the free music shows on offer at this modern venue. You might see a solo cellist or a local DJ or even a Russian folk-punk band. The Maison hosts up to three acts a night, too, so even on a single day there's plenty to choose from. Widen your jazz-overloaded horizons here for the price of a drink. Thoroughly recommended. (508 Frenchmen Street, 504-371-5543, www.maisonfrenchmen.com).

Banks Street Bar and Grill

Not all the best free music is downtown. If you're out and about in Mid City, you'll find a friendly welcome and some smoking hot bands and musicians at this rocking little joint. There's sometimes free food as well, but take your chances anyway (4401 Banks Street, 504-486-0258, www.banksstreetbarandgrill.com).

House of Blues

New Orleans' biggest downtown music venue has some of the best-known bands in the country passing through, and it likes to share the wealth by opening up its smaller rooms for free music showcases. Dates and times can vary, but look out for the nights where they open up Big Mama's Lounge, which hosts regular free performances (225 Decatur Street, 504-310-4999, www.houseofblues.com).

BJ's Lounge

One of the most popular free music nights is on a Monday night in this Bywater dive bar. King James and The Special Men are a beloved local band, and play a weekly residency here to a smoky, booze-filled, adoring crowd. Expect to rub shoulders with hipsters and locals, enjoy cheap drinks and a packed dance floor (4310 Burgundy).

Neutral Ground Coffee House

Head uptown for the city's oldest coffee shop, and to experience something a little different by way of musical entertainment. Mostly a folk and acoustic music venue, Neutral Ground hosts free live music seven nights a week, and their calendar boasts weekly regulars, open mic spots and visiting artists. The venue is alcohol and smoke free (5110 Danneel Street, 504-891-3381, www.neutralgroundcoffeehouse.com).

Blue Nile Open Ears Music Series

One of the oldest jazz clubs in the city – and the oldest building on Frenchmen Street - waives its cover charge every Tuesday night, giving you a chance to take in a diverse range of bands, playing everything from modern jazz to improvised afro-beats. Really a great chance to see some big local names as well as emerging stars (532 Frenchmen St, 504-948-2583, www.bluenilelive.com).

Wednesdays on the Point

During the summer months, you can take the ferry to Algiers Point on the West Bank in the later afternoon for a laid back series of excellent concerts. Sit back with a drink and enjoy local brass bands and jazz singers with the New Orleans skyline as a backdrop and the

Mississippi River stretched out before you. Not too shabby (www.wednesdaysonthepoint.com).

Foundation Free Fridays, Tipitinas

The slow summer months are also a great time to head uptown to one of the city's favourite venues. The promoters pull in some big names, and it's well worth leaving downtown for. Funky brass bands are always a major component of the line up, but whoever's playing, it's all free and it's all good (501 Napoleon Avenue, 504-895-8477, www.tipitinas.com).

Jazz in the Park, Louis Armstrong Park

The preservation group People United for Armstrong Park have worked wonders in bringing Spring and Fall seasons of free concerts to this well-loved park. Each Thursday over nine or so weeks, the park turns into a mini-festival ground, with food stalls and vendors and a large stage, where wonderfully eclectic programmes are presented completely free of charge. Each week has at least two acts, and the days last from 2pm to 8pm (North Rampart Street, www.pufap.org).

Wednesday At The Square / Harvest The Music

The square in question is Lafayette Square (on St. Charles Avenue in the CBD), and each March and September sees a 12-week run of weekly concerts organised by the Young Leadership Council. The concerts take place every Wednesday from 5pm-8pm and cover musical ground from brass bands to gospel to rock. There are food stalls and handicrafts for sale, but the music is all free (Lafayette Square, 504-585-1500, www.wednesdayatthesquare.com / www.harvestthemusic.org).

Some other venues that regularly feature free music (check local listings for details) include: The Allways Lounge, Checkpoint Charlies, The Balcony Music Club, and almost every bar on Bourbon Street, though these are mostly loud rock covers bands and bad karaoke).

Free dance lessons

With great music comes great dancing, and New Orleans is awash with dancers of all kinds. They want nothing more than for you to join them, and you'll find free dance lessons almost every night of the week at one venue or another. These free classes are perfect for beginners or those that need to brush up on their skills, and there's usually a themed music night directly following so that you can put your newly-learned moves to the test. Lose your inhibitions, find your rhythm and cut a rug with the locals, all for free.

NOLA Jitterbugs Dance School

This school for learning swing hosts a number of free lesson nights at various bars around the city. At the time of writing, the schedule was:

Sundays: **DBA** at 5pm (618 Frenchmen Street, 504-942-3731, www.dbaneworleans.com)

Sundays: **AllWays Lounge** at 8pm (2240 St Claude Avenue, 504-218-5778, www.theallwayslounge.net)

Mondays: **Mimi's in the Marigny** at 8.30pm (2601 Royal Street, 504-872-9868, www.mimisinthemarigny.net)

Wednesdays: **The Spotted Cat** at 5pm (623 Frenchmen Street, 504-943-3887, www.spottedcatmusicclub.com)

NOLA Jitterbugs Dance School: 2372 St Claude Avenue, 504-383-5284, www.nolajitterbugs.com

There are other free dance lessons available across the city:

Sundays: Salsa at **Mojito's**, 8pm. (437 Esplanade Avenue, 504-252-4800, www.mojitosnola.com)

Mondays: African and Hip Hop at **Ashe CAC**, 6pm. (1712 Oretha C Haley Blvd, 504-569-9070, www.ashecac.org)

Mondays: Swing at **Mojito's**, 8.30pm. (437 Esplanade Avenue, 504-252-4800, www.mojitosnola.com)

Tuesdays: Tango at **Eiffel Society**, 7pm. (2040 St Charles Avenue, 504-525-2951)

Tuesdays: Zydeco at **Rock n' Bowl**, 7pm. (3000 South Carrollton Avenue, 504-861-1700, www.rocknbowl.com)

Tuesdays: Line Dancing at **Mags 940**, 8pm. (940 Elysian Fields, 504-948-1888)

Wednesdays: Line Dancing at **Bullet's**, 6.30pm. (2441 AP Tureaud Avenue, 504-669-4464)

Wednesdays: Swing at **Rock n' Bowl**, 8.30pm. (3000 South Carrollton Avenue, 504-861-1700, www.rocknbowl.com)

Thursdays: African and Hip Hop at **Ashe CAC**, 6pm. (1712 Oretha C Haley Blvd, 504-569-9070, www.ashecac.org)

Fridays: Salsa at **Mojito's**, 8pm. (437 Esplanade Avenue, 504-252-4800, www.mojitosnola.com)

Musical resources

Local radio station **WWOZ** (90.7 FM) is a great resource for all things jazz. Check out their **Livewire Music Event Calendar** for a list of music events (many often free) happening in the city.

Free magazine **Offbeat** (see **Free Resources**) can be picked up in most bars, coffee shops and cafes, and has listings for all the major music venues as well as interviews with the leading lights of the local music scene.

5. FREE EATS AND DRINKS

It's a tough choice deciding whether music or food and drink is the lifeblood of New Orleans. Tune into any local's conversation and – if they're not telling you about what they're eating that minute, they'll tell you what they just ate or what they're about to eat. Add to this the endless debates about where the best Po Boy sandwiches, fried oysters or jambalaya is and you've got yourself a city that's completely obsessed with what it consumes.

"You are not generally helping the local economy by going to Starbucks, McDonald's, Gordon Birsch or Krystal and the like. You come to a town with 3,300 restaurants, and you go to Jamba Juice? Really?"

The good news for you? The city is so proud of its culinary traditions (no other destination in America shows its character through its food in quite the same way) that it is often willing to share it with you for free. I for one have never been anywhere where there is quite the volume of high quality free food on offer for those who know where to look. Rice and beans, barbecue, sandwiches, gumbo, king cake – you can chow down to your heart's (and more likely belly's) content, often for no more than the price of a drink.

Free game day food

Sports fans, you are the luckiest people in town, because come the days when the New Orleans Saints are playing, lots of bars roll out the free snacks in order to get you to sit and drink for three hours. Again, it's a rare neighbourhood bar that doesn't offer SOMETHING in the way of culinary refreshments as they cheer on the black and gold, but among the most celebrated are:

Pal's Lounge

Not only does this Mid City favourite offer free bar food (such as hot dogs and chilli) on game days (including the bigger college ball games), but it also has free red beans and rice on Monday nights (949 Rendon Street, 504-488-7257, www.palslounge.com).

Henry's Uptown Bar

Known as something of a quintessential locals bar, it also offers free BBQ during Saints games (5101 Magazine Street, 504-324-8140).

NOLA Brewing Co. Tap Room

This dog-friendly bar has some great free jambalaya when you buy a drink during Saints games (3001 Tchoupitoulas Steet, 504-301-0117, www.nolabrewing.com).

Robert's Bar

The free ping-pong and pool tables draw a loyal student crowd, and locals join them in numbers for the free barbecue on game days (3125 Calhoun Street, 504- -866-9121).

Kingpin

Not only is there the requisite free game day food at this Elvis-themed bar, but on Friday and Saturday night, cheap food trucks stop by (1307 Lyons Street, 504-891-2373, www.kingpinbar.com).

Finn Mccools Irish Pub

Traditional free game day food, but with the twist of it being more of a pot luck, where the locals bring their own dished to share. Buy your bar neighbour a drink and they'll likely let you have your fill of whatever it was they bought. If you want to get creative, you can win a free bar tab if you bring a dish and it's chosen as the best of the day (3701 Banks Street, 504-486-9080, www.finnmccools.com).

"We love visiting sports fans, but use your common sense. Try not to loudly berate the locals in their own bars. We're all for some sporting banter, but remember you're a visitor and don't get aggressively competitive. We drink as much when we lose as when we win, and we'll mostly be great sports about it."

General free food

Even if you're not a sports fan – and we understand that at least SOME people of this persuasion exist in this city – you can pick up some great free food if you're happy to patronise the right establishment on the right night. Again, you're likely to have to shell out for the odd drink, but we think you're still getting a great deal of free hospitality. The following were all on offer at the time of writing – if you're making a special trip then of course it makes sense to call ahead and check, because things can change fast here (sometimes, at least...).

Handsome Willy's

There's a pretty good revolving choice of free food every Friday night, coinciding with Happy Hour, which is 5pm-9pm. Expect BBQ, burgers, tacos, etc. (218 S. Robertson Street, 504-525-0377, www.handsomewillys.com).

Mick's Irish Pub

A wealth of free food happens here, starting with traditional rice and beans on Mondays, then anything from hot dogs to sandwiches through to Friday. As they like to say: "Weekends, you're on your own." (4801 Bienville Street, 504-482-9113, www.mickspub.com)

Rendezvous Tavern

There's a rare chance to try Indian food in New Orleans here every Sunday afternoon, with spicy curries and exotic sides from local Indian restaurant Nirvana. (3101 Magazine Street, 504-891-1777)

J&J's Sports Lounge

According to several locals, locals bring free side dishes into the bar at the weekends, and not exclusively for game days, though this is perhaps when the best choice might be found (800 France Street, 504-942-8877).

R Bar

This Marigny staple has regular Free Food Fridays, which can be as exciting as a crawfish boil in season. You're encouraged to tip the chef. And drink, of course (1431 Royal Street, 504-948-7499)

Le Bon Temp Roule

Locals say head uptown early for the free Friday night oysters as they go pretty quickly. You can stay for the free live music even if you miss out. The seafood comes out at 7pm. (4801 Magazine Street, 504-895-8117)

Banks Street Bar and Grill

"Banks St. Bar has 'Spaghetti Western Sunday's'. There's free BBQ, good old school country music played by Ron Hotstream and they show a

spaghetti western as they do it." (4401 Banks Street, 504-486-0258, www.banksstreetbarandgrill.com).

International Society for Krishna Consciousness

If you don't want to sit in a bar and drink to get free food, then the Sunday Night Love Feast at the local Hare Krishna temple is a free meal for everyone that shows up. Food is served at 5.30pm and there are discussions and prayers from 6pm (2936 Esplanade Avenue, www.iskcon-nola.org).

Free drinks

For a boozy city, free drinks are kind of harder to come by, but you do have a couple of options if making friends with the locals or getting yourself invited to a party proves too much effort (side note: this should not be too much effort, and buying drinks for visitors who prove themselves decent people is one of New Orleans' favourite pastimes. Be nice and you shall be rewarded, esteemed travelling friend). Your free drink options mostly centre around wine tastings, so you're not going to be able to bowl up and just get loaded for free, but you may get to taste some nice wine and have some conversation and make friends. So you're getting a lot for essentially no money.

Swirl Wine Bar and Market

Friday nights are busy because of 'Friday Free For All', whereby the owners kindly let you sample four varieties of wine for free AND they serve up cheap tapas to go with them, so you're well looked after (3143 Ponce de Leon Street, 504-304-0635, www.swirlinthecity.com).

Pearl Wine Company

These wine buffs offer two opportunities to taste wine for free, on Thursdays from 5pm to 7pm and on Fridays at the same times. But that's not all: on Tuesdays from 5pm they offer free red beans and rice, and on Wednesdays, they have ten wines by the glass for just $5 each (3700 Orleans Avenue, 504-483-6314, www.pearlwineco.com).

Bacchanal

I'm not aware of anyone ever having had a bad time at Bachannal, an out-of-the-way wine bar in the far reaches of the Bywater. As well as being an all-round great idea (live music in a lovely courtyard with an amazing wine list – what's not to like?), they also do free wine tastings every Saturday afternoon from 3pm (600 Poland Avenue, 504-948-9111, www.bacchanalwine.com).

Martin Wine Cellar

This wine merchants has multiple locations around the city and the suburbs, and runs pretty regular free Friday wine tastings, usually from around 4.30pm-6.30pm. Check their website for upcoming events and locations (www.martinwinecellar.com).

Harrah's Casino

If you're thinking of gambling, you can of course sit at the machines or the tables of the casino and in theory you'll get free drinks as long as you're playing. Tips and potential losses make this a risky enterprise if you're just in it for the drinks, but if you're gambling anyway, you're in luck (228 Poydras Street, 1-800-427-7247, www.harrahsneworleans.com).

Free corkage

A certain number of restaurants in New Orleans allow you take in your own bottle of wine, and further more, are kind enough not to charge you a corkage fee. We'd make this observation: it won't look too good if you roll up with a five dollar bottle, nor particularly great if it's a bottle that's on the restaurant's wine list. The best idea is to call ahead, but with that said, here are the no-corkage-fee restaurants:

Restaurant August (301 Tchoupitoulas St, 504-299-9777)
Arnaud's (813 Bienville Ave, 504-523-5433)
Bennachin (1212 Royal St, 504-522-1230)
Bistro Daisy (5831 Magazine St, 504-899-6987) – no fee for 1st two bottles, then $15/bottle
Eat New Orleans (900 Dumaine St, 504-522-7222) – no fee for 1st bottle, then $15/bottle
La Macarena Pupuseria (8120 Hampson St, 504-862-5252)
Lebanon's Café (1500 S. Carrollton Ave, 504-862-6200)
Le Meritage (1001 Toulouse St, 504-522-8800) – no fee at lunch
Luke (333 St Charles Ave, 504-524-8890) – no fee
Magasin Cafe (4201 Magazine St, 504-896-7611) – no fee

Martin Wine Cellar (3500 Magazine St, 504-894-7420) – no fee
Martinique Bistro (5908 Magazine St, 504-891-8495) – no fee on Tuesdays
Mona's Cafe (4126 Magazine St, 504-894-9800) – no fee

There are a few restaurants that allow you to bring your own bottles for a nominal corkage charge. Among them are **SukhoThai** (1913 Royal Stree, 504-948-9309, www.sukhothai-nola.com), **Dante's Kitchen** (736 Dante Street, 504-861-3121, www.danteskitchen.com), **Eat New Orleans** (900 Dumaine Street, 504-522-7222, www.eatnola.com), and **Gott Gourmet Café** (3100 Magazine Street, 504-373- 6579, www.gottgourmetcafe.com).

Some miscellaneous free food and drink tips:

Community Coffee (multiple locations across the city, www.communitycoffee.com) offer free same-day refills on selected sizes and drinks.

It's not strictly a free meal, but you'll likely get some tasty samples **at Crescent City Farmer's Market**, especially if you belly up to one of their free cookery demonstrations (700 Magazine Street, 504-861-4488).

You'll find there's plenty of free food on offer around **Crawfish Season** (March through June as a rough rule of thumb). Many bars around the city do their own crawfish boils, and offer patrons free mudbugs (or charge a token amount) as long as they're drinking. So you can fill up easily on seafood, potatoes and corn on the cob – just ask a local how to take those tasty morsels apart to get to the meat.

Honourable mentions:

You'll really want to catch some of the city's best musicians while you're here, and some of them put on some free food for those that pay the cover charge. Notable nights include **Vaughn's Lounge** (4229 Dauphine Street, 504-947-5562) on Thursday nights for local legend Kermit Ruffins' set and the **Candlelight Lounge** (925 N Robertson Street, 504-525-4748, www.candlelightlounge.net) on Wednesdays when the excellent Tremé Brass Band plays. Kermit

Ruffins also stars in his own night at **Bullet's Sports Bar** (2441 AP Tureaud Avenue, 504-669-4464) with his own band, the Barbecue Swingers. There's a cover, but there's also some extremely cheap BBQ from the stall outside, and is likely more than you can eat for just a few dollars.

The **Hi-Ho Lounge** (2239 St Claude, 504-945-4446, www.hiholounge.net) has very affordable two dollar rice and beans on Monday nights.

Several people have told me that their favourite Happy Hour for food was the one at **Domenica** (123 Baronne Street, 504-648-6020, www.domenicarestaurant.com). At the time of writing, the deal was half price on all pizzas, wines by the glass, cocktails and beers, 3pm-6pm, seven days a week. I've been many times and it's outstandingly good value.

Commander's Palace (1403 Washington Avenue, 504-899-8221, www.commanderspalace.com) is a higher end restaurant, BUT as one local points out, this is a pretty good deal: *"If you're eating at Commander's Palace, go for lunch and take advantage of their 25¢ martinis."*

Delachaise (3442 St Charles Avenue, 504-895-0858, www.thedelachaise.com), one of our favourite Garden District drinking spots, has daily $5 wine specials and a fine line in small plates.

And some words of wisdom for saving money on your eating out bill in general: *"There is little difference in quality between the food at the "famous" expensive restaurants and the more 'dive-y' ones like Liuzzas at the Track and Buffas. Eat like a local."*

Some free drinking advice:

"Don't drink too much on the first night. Pace yourself."

"If your entertainment style is all shots, breasts and "Totes YOLO, dude! WOOOOOH!" find Bourbon Street and stay there."

"Don't carry your hand grenade cup uptown with you, folks get judgemental and cabs will subtly cost more."

"There is no race or rush in the land of no 'Last Call.' You call it moderation, we call it endurance."

Cheers.

6. MARDI GRAS

Yes, it gets its own section, it being one of, if not THE biggest free party on the planet. Again, advice on making the most of this sprawling, multi-faceted festival could take up an entire book. There are lots of resources that will explain Mardi Gras to the uninitiated, so we'll try and keep to the insider's path – for a primer, I'd recommend going to www.mardigrasneworleans.com, where the history, traditions and schedules are all laid out.

At the time of writing, there were 62 official parades (all free of course), stretching across a month's time period leading up to Fat Tuesday (in French, *Mardi Gras* – see?). They take place all over the city, some in the suburbs and beyond and there can be as many as ten parades a day, from the huge 'super krewes' (the organisations that organise parades are known as 'krewes') to small, boutique marches in quiet neighbourhoods that only a few people take part in. Again, the above website will help you choose which ones you'll want to see – everyone from dog owners to sports fans to sci-fi nerds are catered for, so don't worry about that.

People line the parade routes early – often turning up hours before start time for the bigger parades (which usually happen uptown). They're there to see the floats and costumes, of course, but they're also trying to get a good spot to catch the 'throws' that the people on the floats will toss out into the crowds. These are plastic toys and trinkets – usually Mardi Gras beads – but they can also be more elaborate, special prizes that are highly valued. The Krewe of Muses, for example, hands out a limited number of glamorously-customised shoes, and people will clamour energetically for these exotic rewards.

"Get into the spirit, but don't get ridiculous about catching parade throws. If you're grabbing a plastic toy out of the hands of a young child, you need to calm down. That kid will appreciate the toy way more than you will in five minutes' time. Be a decent human. Share the wealth with those less able to jump up for the throws."

Forget your preconceptions about how raunchy and wild it is. There may be the odd college girl taking her top off on Bourbon Street, but most of the parades are incredibly family friendly, and many of them are geared especially towards children having a good time. If you know a local, or make friends with any, chances are they'll be setting up a picnic on the sidewalk or on the grassy median strip – known as 'neutral grounds'.

Whether you have children or not, even the most cursory attempt to get a throw will be rewarded eventually - by the end, you'll have more beads and toys than you care to carry. The krewes also throw out huge plastic bags and cups, and these are really worth grabbing so you can carry your haul around and grab a drink if anyone offers you one. The cups last pretty well and make great souvenirs. Also look out for doubloons (gold coins), glow sticks and beer coozies flying across your path. It's not strictly in the tradition to grab things off the floor, but people won't judge you too harshly if it's something worth picking up.

The most important thing: COSTUME.

Locals really appreciate your going to the effort of dressing up for this free party they throw every year. The wilder the better, and you can pretty much wander round in costume from about a week before Fat Tuesday. Lundi Gras (Monday) is a very big costume day, and the day itself is an obvious chance to shine. Again, you can pick up great free accessories and beads by just turning up to the parades and claiming throws.

It's impossible to list all the free things you'll get at Mardi Gras. People will give you drinks and food and hugs and the run of their houses. You just have to open yourself up to the experience and throw yourself into the spirit of it. If you do, you'll get the greatest thing in the world for free: a truly unforgettable experience.

Free Mardi Gras advice:

"Don't be that guy during Mardi Gras shouting at every girl you see to show you their breasts. It really doesn't happen that much outside of Bourbon Street. Be respectful."

"Pace yourself. Oh man. Pace yourself."

"Make some uptown friends who have a house near the parade route because the old line from the song is true – there's nowhere to pee on Mardi Gras."

"Get into costume beyond a yellow, purple and gold polo shirt. We all appreciate even the smallest effort to make it look like you're part of our favourite celebration."

A free story: How to Mardi Gras like a local by someone who isn't a local. That would be me.

"*If you go to New Orleans,*" musical legend Professor Longhair repeatedly told me as I idled in my basement apartment in London, "*You ought to go see the Mardi Gras.*"

Reader, I took him up on that tasty but somewhat obvious morsel of advice, and as a regular visitor to this fine city, I annually joined the throngs, hordes and thoroughly-beaded hoi polloi at America's biggest party.

I jockeyed for position in the scrums along Saint Charles and Canal, roared at Rex, bawled at Bacchus and got caught in the maul for footwear at Muses. In short, I had a similarly great Mardi Gras experience to almost everybody else that brings their bright-eyed selves into town for Carnival.

Then I moved here.

Now, don't get me wrong. I know, it's the accent - it's easy to misunderstand - but let me be clear. I love the sheer spectacle of the huge, gaily lumbering mega krewes, the vast floats and gigantic cacophony.

But as a local – albeit an honorary one – I wanted to mix in something more personal. I had friends here now. There was intimacy. I wanted Mardi Gras days brimming over with unique moments, to be personally romanced as opposed to overwhelmed by a showboat the size of a several cruise liners.

This takes investment. Effort, even - if getting up to drink preparatory mimosas at 7.30am before joining the early-morning march of the Krewe of St Anne (or the Societé de Sainte Anne to give it its formal name) can be dubbed such a thing.

As my merry band blearily made our way to Bud Rips on Piety Street in the Bywater, a trickle of daybreak revellers became a stream and then a lake. It's 8.30am and champagne bottles are being passed between intricately-costumed weirdoes, throwing caution to the wind and starting Mardi Gras day at full tilt.

By the time the march, lead by the ebullient Storyville Stompers band, reaches R Bar on Royal, I'm heady with music and colours and, obviously, booze. I've already had several smile-inducing personal moments, including a conversation with a toddler dressed as Einstein.

No matter that I don't fully partake in the full tradition of St Anne – the onward march to see Rex, the observance of pouring ashes of loved ones into the river, even this small *amuse bouche* of a lesser-known parade has whet my appetite.

Here's where the delicious treasures are. In the grubby nooks between, under and behind the grand krewes. I don't doubt the grandstanders' commitment for a second, but in the micro-krewes, the nerdcore marches and the niche celebrations, you find carnivalistic zeal bar none.

Of course, the purists will seek out the Mardi Gras Indians. They are slightly less mysterious than they previously were thanks to being a central theme of the HBO show *Treme*. However, they are still cloaked in mystery that's as elaborate and beautiful as their huge, feathery creations, worn through the streets on Mardi Gras Day amid strict historical observances. The Big Chief is barely visible under his regal finery, his flag boys and spy boys whooping to warn of encroaching rivalries.

New mixes with old in subversive ways in the backstreets during Mardi Gras. 'Captain' Oscar Diggs of krewedelusion says people seeking them out on the last Saturday before Mardi Gras will see them "taking the time-honored conceit of Carnival royalty and follow it to its most literal and absurd endpoint." This generally means brutal satire and secretive practices via the mind of their infamous 'Enlightened Despot', Davis Rogan.

An early celebration of sisterhood lies in the nascent mobile oestrogenics of the Krewe of Goddesses. "We stand by the philosophy that every woman is a Goddess," says co founder Kimberley Gondrella. "We represent creative, inspirational and sexually empowered women and the men who love and support them."

Marching alongside krewe*delusion* you'll find women from all walks of life, from lawyers to designers to burlesque dancers. An annual oyster bash is being touted as their culinary tradition, decorated oyster shells as well as hand-customised panties being their throws of choice.

There's fanaticism at work here, to be sure, ones that reward their fans and those that stumble upon them with an intoxicating mix of whimsy and creativity. One that has captured imaginations in recent years has been the Intergalactic Krewe of Chewbacchus – their mission, "To save the universe, one drunken nerd at a time."

OK, so you may not recognise exactly which minor Star Wars character is being parodied, but there is, in common with all the minor, niche krewes, a sense of their own ridiculousness, and this oozes inclusivity. By laughing at us and with us, you're laughing at yourself, and that's the true spirit of Carnival.

One of the most touching and memorable parades I saw last year was one I almost had to squint to see. The 'titRex parade (a play on Petit Rex) is almost heartbreaking in its concept and execution.

Stand on the right corners of the Marigny at the right times and you'll see a cavalcade of the most touching shoebox floats, all fully articulate and blooming with miniature, detailed farce and a beaming, proud designer pulling it along on its string.

It's hard to think of a more culinary parade than the Red Beans n' Rice. Monday – Lundi Gras – is of course the appropriate day to see this "bean-centric second line". Camellia beans are meticulously glued to suits, and the wanton legume-ry sees a parade with the Treme Brass Band through Marigny and Treme neighbourhoods. Catch them and you too can say "Bean there, done that."

I don't know exactly what Fess wants me to see at Mardi Gras other than Zulu. I'm not doubting the wisdom of such an esteemed voice on the subject. I'm just saying that as much as I've joyously revelled in the majesty of the mega-krewes, it's the smaller, more exotic bites that have stuck in my teeth. If you want to help me make memories this year, I'll see you outside Bud Rips early on Mardi Gras morning.

7. FREE FESTIVALS

Outside of the small matter of Mardi Gras, New Orleans spices up its year with a wealth of free festivals. Even these free ones attract some big local players, so don't discount them at all. There are some good ones that you can buy tickets for (Jazz Fest, Voodoo Fest), but luckily for you, there are even more that don't cost a dime to attend. They mostly centre around large music stages, and so you can easily just wander into whatever neighbourhood they're in and set yourself down to enjoy the show.

French Quarter Festival (mid April)

Dedicated to the musical community of NOLA, this festival is growing quickly and is already some people's favourite time outside of Mardi Gras. I've heard more than one person refer to it as 'the true local's festival', so you can consider yourself in the know if you rock up for this one. At last count, some 1,400 musicians played over the long weekend. All local, and covering everything from Jazz to Zydeco. Four days. 400 hours of free music. Your only costs are food and drink. You lucky, lucky people (www.fqfi.org).

Satchmo Summer Fest (early August)

Truth be told, the summer months are kind of tough in New Orleans. The humid weather sets in, people get out of town and it just gets kind of quiet. The people that stay need something to do, and so lo and behold, Satchmo Summer Fest was born. It honours the city's favourite son, of course: Louis 'Satchmo' Armstrong, and includes second line parades, jazz masses, dance lessons and of course, music stages around the French Quarter (www.fqfi.org/satchmosummerfest).

The Crescent City BBQ and Blues Festival (mid October)

Not all festivals take place in the historic Quarter. Some happen in the not-so-historic-but-nevertheless-charming CBD (Central Business District). Just before the madness of Halloween, two stages go up around Lafayette Square and for two full days, some really big international names and a wealth of local talent line up to entertain the masses for free, bought to you by the New Orleans Jazz & Heritage Festival (www.jazzandheritage.org/blues-fest).

Congo Square New World Rhythms Festival (late March)

The New Orleans Jazz & Heritage Festival also brings you a little somethin'-somethin' in Spring, arguably the nicest time to be in New Orleans. The city is recovering from its collective Mardi Gras hangover and Congo Square (in Louis Armstrong Park on Rampart Street) brightens up the city once more with a full weekend of the music and dance of Africa, the Caribbean, the American Gulf South and beyond (www.jazzandheritage.org/congo-square).

Tremé Creole Gumbo Festival (early November)

Yet ANOTHER free celebration from The New Orleans Jazz & Heritage Festival. They really spoil you, you know? The Treme Creole Gumbo Festival celebrates what it calls "the melting-pot culture of New Orleans" and you can see brass bands and New Orleans jazz aplenty. If you're more interested in the 'cooking pot culture' of the city, you'll also find a huge selection of the best gumbo in town (www.jazzandheritage.org/treme-gumbo).

Louisiana Cajun-Zydeco Festival (mid June)

The final free festival from the good folks at The New Orleans Jazz & Heritage Festival (it's almost too good to be true how much they give away for free – are we sure there's no catch?) rounds off the musical story of the city. Again on stages in Armstrong Park, the lively strains of Cajun and Zydeco bands delight locals and visitors for an entire weekend (www.jazzandheritage.org/cajun-zydeco).

NOLA Navy Week (mid April)

This is a commemoration of the war of 1812, and is marked with a spectacle of historic tall ships (and some modern day equivalents) sailing along and docking at the East Bank of the Mississippi River, from Erato Street to Upper Poland Avenue. The Navy's Blue Angels air display team also fly over and perform a daring air show as part of the week's festivities (www.nolanavyweek.com).

Vieux to Do (mid June)

This is actually the convergence of three free festivals: The Creole Tomato Festival, the New Orleans Seafood Festival, and the Louisiana Cajun-Zydeco Festival. They take over the Vieux Carré (French Quarter) for a weekend, and celebrate – respectively – one of the region's most vital ingredients, the indigenous musical traditions of this part of the world and, not least, the best-loved local oceanic produce (www.frenchmarket.org)

Bayou Boogaloo (mid May)

Conceived to help a neighbourhood revive itself after Katrina, this free music and arts event has gone from strength to strength and draws crowds of around 35,000 to the banks of the Bayou. As well as the main stages, there is a kids' stage and art demonstrations from some of the city's most creative folk (www.thebayouboogaloo.com).

Freret Street Festival (early April)

A couple of years ago, this was a pretty desolate part of town. Now it's one of the city's most up and coming neighbourhoods, and this resurgence has supported this free music and arts festival, which runs for about six blocks. Live bands, kids' activities Mardi Gras Indians and brass bands delight the uptown crowds (www.freretstreetfestival.com).

White Linen Night (early August)

Traditional summer formal wear is almost mandatory at this Warehouse District event, which highlights the art galleries in and around this neighbourhood. Many of them set up stalls and hand out free hand held fans and glasses of wine as the smartly-dressed crowds peruse the works on display. There are also small stages with local musicians (www.cacno.org).

Dirty Linen Night (mid August)

White Linen Night is parodied in the French Quarter, and galleries here open up their doors in unison, offering exhibitions and drinks to all comers. It's a much less formal affair than its sister event, so choose which one suits your speed. Or go to both (see local listings).

PhotoNOLA (mid December)

New Orleans is such a visually striking city that it's no surprise that a talented and inspiring photographic community thrives here. Every year, galleries open their doors and show off the best of the year's works, and there are free exhibitions at varied venues across the city, from arts centres to coffee shops (www.photonola.org).

Halloween (late October)

OK, so this isn't an actual festival, but after Mardi Gras, it's the time you'll see the most locals in states of costuming, so it kind of feels like one. Maybe because of its historic backdrop and the ghost tours of the French Quarter, but Halloween celebrations in NOLA just feel right. And boy, so the locals throw themselves into the spirit (no pun intended) of things. If it falls on a weekend, you can expect parades and zombie walks and even miniature krewes handing out candy or throws. In short, it's a great time to be around the city and you can partake in the spooky atmosphere for free just walking around the Quarter.

St Patrick's Day (mid March) / Day of the Dead (early November)/ Running of the Bulls (mid July) / Bastille Day (mid July)

Depending on your views about co-opting a cultural celebration from another country, these can also be fun times to be in NOLA. Most people's views are: it's yet another chance to dress up and drink. They all involve free parades and spectacles and there's likely a free music stage going on somewhere. They are as they are in their native countries but smaller (and in the case of the running of the bulls, the bulls are women on roller skates, so arguably less dangerous).

Honourable mentions

Greek Fest (late May)

Organised around Memorial Day Weekend, this celebration of all things Hellenic (www.greekfestnola.com) takes place along the shores of Lake Pontchartrain in the shadow of the Greek Cathedral. There are family-friendly attractions, music and a wealth of authentic foods, and entrance is just $5 (www.greekfestnola.com).

New Orleans Fringe Festival (mid-late November)

From small beginnings, this theatrical celebration now sees more than 70 acts from the city and all over the country (with the odd international act thrown in) descend on venues from large theatres to coffee shops to people's houses and stage all manner of drama, comedy, dance, mime, musicals and puppetry. And the best thing? Tickets are just $8 per show, so you can afford to be daring and broaden your horizons somewhat (www.nofringe.org).

8. FREE TOURS

We all like a little local knowledge, and there's nothing like a tour for some fast-track insider information. New Orleans is really a city of tour guides – talk to almost any local and they'll likely instantly turn into a knowledgeable ambassador for NOLA. It's almost a point of pride in these parts. But if you want something a bit more specific than where you bar neighbour likes to eat Po-Boys, then you can take any of the following tours for free. Noted, some of them are self guided, but with a little reading, it can still feel like an educational and entertaining (edu-taining?) afternoon out.

St Louis Cathedral

It's the building that dominates the low-rise skyline of the French Quarter, surrounded as it is by bars and Bourbon Street and street trumpeters and tarot card readers. It's well worth ducking into, though, and although there are no official tours, you could well be lucky. This, from the cathedral's website: "The Cathedral is open daily after the 7:30 am mass until 4:00 pm. Self-guided brochures are available in the entrance for a $1.00 donation. Visitors can get an impromptu tour from our volunteer docents when available. Guided tours for groups are only available with prior reservations." So now you know (615 Pere Antoine Alley, 504-525-9585, www.stlouiscathedral.org).

New Orleans Lager and Ale Brewing Company

Of course, it's arguable that alcohol is the true religion of this city. For a closer look at one of the local brews, you can join a free tour of the facility every Friday at 2pm. You do, of course, need to be 21 years of age or above. The best thing, though, is that there's a free tasting at the end of the tour (which lasts about an hour if you're trying to gauge your thirst levels). 3001 Tchoupitoulas, 504-301-0117, www.nolabrewing.com.

Cemeteries

Grab a map from any of the tourist offices (e.g. the one at 600 Decatur Street) and treat yourself to a self-guided tour of the city's famous tombs. There are guided tours available, but unless you have very specific questions, you can do more or less as well under your own steam. If you only explore one of the cemeteries, make it St. Louis Cemetery No. #1 on Basin Street - the final resting place of Voodoo Queen Marie Laveau. Some ESSENTIAL free advice: Never go to the cemeteries after dark – stick to daylight hours, when other people are around.

Literary NOLA

The Crescent City has long been a magnet for some of the world's most talented and decadent writers. It doesn't take must to work out your own route and walk in the footsteps of literary greats such as Tennessee Williams, William Faulkner, Truman Capote, Thornton Wilder, Walker Percy, and Anne Rice. Google your favourite writers and then work their landmarks into a self-guided walking tour – Frommer's Guide Books have some great suggested routes: http://www.frommers.com/destinations/new-orleans/717264

Honourable mention

Historic New Orleans Collection

Now, this museum and collection of buildings and exhibits chronicling the cultural history of New Orleans (see FREE MUSUEUMS, below), does offer free self-guided tours. For some real insight, though, it's worth paying the $5 for the docent-guided public tour, which will help bring the museum to life even more. Tours are daily: Tuesday–Saturday; 10am, 11am, 2pm, 3pm. Sunday: 11am, 2pm, 3pm. Call ahead for reservations.

533 Royal Street, 504 523 4662, www.hnoc.org

Free local advice on undertaking a self tour of the city:

"While you may be given the impression by your tour guides that the Quarter is like an adult Disneyland, please keep in mind that people do actually live there. Taking photographs through windows, over walls and through gates is frowned upon. An especially big no-no is taking photographs of that girl sat on her balcony in her pyjamas trying to

enjoy her morning tea in peace. Seriously. Ask nicely and they'll probably give you permission."

"Never ask for 'north,' you're on a semi-cardinal grid in the Quarter, in a near concentric-city. Ask to/from: River, St. Louis Cathedral, Superdome, Lake, Uptown, Marigny, City Park, Audubon Park. Get a map that has the Quarter in detail, AND one of the city from Metairie line to Arabi, Lake to Algiers Point, preferably on the flip-side of the Quarter-Map."

"Unless there is a road block, the French Quarter is not pedestrian mall. Walk on the sidewalk and NOT in the middle of the street."

9. FREE MUSEUMS

Let's face it, the entire city is something of a living museum. Almost every building in the French Quarter is an exhibit in itself and the fact that people actually live there helps keep it alive. In truth, nobody really comes to New Orleans for the museums. Nevertheless, we have some good ones, and you can still see some bona fide history and art without dipping into your pockets. You just have to know where to look and when to go.

Historic New Orleans Collection

This huddle of historic buildings on Royal Street hides a wealth of culturally important exhibits. It's a museum, a research centre and a local publisher dedicated to studying and, more importantly, preserving the history of NOLA and the Southern Gulf region. The Williams Gallery houses changing exhibitions, while the Louisiana History Galleries have ten rooms of permanent displays. The Williams Residence is a preserved historic house and there is also a gift shop. The collection owns around 35,000 books and 350,000 photos, prints and other artefacts. There are also tours (see honourable mentions in FREE TOURS, above).

533 Royal Street, 504 523 4662, www.hnoc.org

St Mary's Assumption Church

Not strictly a museum but this baroque-style church is home to the National Shrine of Blessed St Francis Xavier Seelos. One of the most beloved holy figures in Lousiana's history. There's an organ that dates back to 1861, 19th-century hand-carved wooden statues, and a tranquil, magnolia-filled courtyard. The Shrine is open Monday-Friday from 9am to 3pm, and Saturday from 10am to 3.30pm. St. Mary's and St. Alphonsus (across the street) are listed on the National Register of Historic Places.

923 Josephine Street, 504 522 6748,
www.stalphonsusneworleans.com

Germaine Cazenave Wells Mardi Gras Museum

As well as having top notch food and an excellent bar (The French 75), Arnuad's Restaurant is also the home to one of the city's lesser-known museums. Walk through the doors at the back of the bar (order a cocktail from bartender to the stars Chris Hannah on the way) and then up the stairs. You'll find a room of glass cabinets showcasing the extravagant costumery of Ms Germaine Cazenave Wells – daughter to Count Arnaud, for whom the restaurant is named. 13 lavish Mardi Gras get-ups grace the walls, along with children's costumes and 70 vintage photos. Hidden treasures, indeed. Open during restaurant hours, seven days a week.

813 Bienville, 504 523 5433, www.arnuadsrestaurant.com

Sydney and Walda Besthoff Sculpture Park

A wonderful collection of over 60 sculptures set in lovely landscaped gardens outside the New Orleans Museum of Art. Among the big name works are those by Henry Moore, Renoir and Magritte. Bring a picnic and lunch among some of scuplting's finest exponents. (1 Collins C. Diboll Circle, City Park, 504 658 4100, www.noma.org).

Honourable mentions

The American Italian Museum

Tucked away in the Warehouse District, the museum details the history of the contribution of the city's Italian Americans. See the Giovanni Schiavo Collection, one of the world's most significant collections of Italian-American history, and marvel at the gown worn by opera singer Marguerite Piazza at the Italian Mardi Gras ball and the St Joseph Day altar display. The museum opens up onto the Piazza d'Italia, a tranquil monument to the Italian-American community. Adult tickets are $8. (537 S. Peters Street, 504 522 1657, www.airf.org).

Both the excellent **Ogden Museum of Southern Art** (925 Camp Street, 504 539 9650, www.ogdenmuseum.org) and the best art museum in the city, **New Orleans Museum of Art** (1 Collins C. Diboll Circle, City Park, 504 658 4100, www.noma.org), have free admission days but at the time of writing, these offers were only extended to Louisiana residents with proof of I.D. So...make friends.

10. FREE ART AND CULTURE

Royal Street, Julia Street, Jackson Square, art markets in Mid City and Bywater...it's not exactly a difficult task tracking down places to look at art for free in New Orleans. Granted, most of the places you'll see it will be trying – though not in an annoying way – to sell it to you, but galleries are so used to people just wandering in off the street, cocktail in hand, that they don't employ the hard sell. A lot of the art is "local" – which mainly means silhouettes of saxophone players leaning against lampposts, but look beyond the obvious tourist traps – at Graphite Gallery on Royal Street or Byrdie's Gallery on Saint Claude - and you'll find a vibrant, inventive and most of all thoroughly modern art scene.

The Arts District
This is a former industrial area from the 19th century, and has flourished ever ever since the Contemporary Arts Center ($5 admission) opened there in 1976. Today, over 25 art galleries line the historic district, most located on Julia Street. Visit the neighbourhood on the first Saturday of each month, when Julia Street has an evening gallery hop and many of the galleries are open for free.

Frenchmen Street Art Market
A former disused lot was reinvented in 2013 as a lovely night market, with strings of lights illuminating a friendly space where local artists peddle their wares. There's everything from original paintings to sculpture to perfumes and jewellery. And the stall holders are usually the person that made what you're looking at, and who love to chat. Open Thursday – Saturday from 7pm until 1am and Sunday 6pm to midnight (619 Frenchmen Street, 504 941 1149, www.frenchmenartmarket.com).

Collins C Diboll Art Gallery
Located on the fourth floor of the J. Edgar and Louise S. Monroe Library at Loyola University, this neat little space hosts a range of student, local, national, and international exhibits throughout the year. There's a peaceful outdoor sculpture garden, and both the art gallery and garden are free to the public (6363 St Charles Avenue, 504 864 7248, www.loyno.edu/dibollgallery).

Free film

New Orleans Film Society

Not everything the NOFS show is free, but they do have a substantial amount of free screenings and it's well worth checking out their website to see what's coming up www.neworleansfilmsociety.org.

Honourable mention

Indywood

This pop-up style cinema is part of a bigger project that aims to promote and sustain the local film making industry, and is run by a couple of passionate young enthusiasts. The cinema concentrates on locally-made films, and you can see some wonderful documentaries in particular. And the best thing: it's a great downtown alternative to the expensive Canal Place option. Tickets just $5 and they show films Thursday through Sunday www.indywood.org.

Zeitgeist

A 'multi-disciplinary arts center', which has been bringing alternative culture to New Orleans since 1986. It's a charmingly lo-fi venue, which screens obscure cult classics and has a nice line in independent European cinema. Tickets are around $8 and you can attend screenings that you really wouldn't see anywhere else in town www.zeitgeist.net.

Free Poetry

All that freeform jazz apparently gave rise to a generation of free-spirited poets, and their legacy lives on in the lively poetry scene in the city. You'll find some of the local poetic types out along Frenchmen Street writing on-the-spot rhymes for busking money, but you can see more formal recitals at these free regular poetry nights:

BJ's Lounge
The Blood Jet Poetry Series runs at 8pm on Wednesdays and mixes

music, poetry and an open mic.
4301 Burgundy Street, www.facebook.com/bloodjetpoetry

Maple Leaf Bar
Founded in 1979, the Everette C. Maddox Memorial Prose and Poetry Reading is at 3pm every Sunday. It is named after a poet who frequented the Maple Leaf Bar, and this weekly event is the longest-running poetry reading in North America, according to the bar.
8316 Oak Street, 504 866 9359, www.mapleleafbar.com

Kajun's Pub
At 7pm on the second Saturday of every month, the **ColdCuts Salon** reading series features poetry and spoken word performances.
2256 St. Claude Avenue, 504 947 3735,
www.coldcutsreading.blogspot.com

Free Fiction

AllWays Lounge
If you don't mind a little raciness with your writing, there's a full night of entertainment on offer at **Esoterotica.** This is a bi-weekly (Wednesday) night show where the local 'provocateurs' read new fiction and poetry to a room of romantics and rascals. Starts at 8pm. (2240, Saint Claude, 504 218 5778, www.theallwayslounge.net).

Free Burlesque

The city has a very strong tradition of this saucy performance discipline. There are several very well-known troops in town, but most of the revues charge a cover. You can see a couple of show for free, though. The most sophisticated is the Burlesque Ballroom, which happens at midnight on Friday at the **Irvin Mayfield Lounge** (Royal Sonesta Hotel, 300 Bourbon Street, 504 553 2299, www.sonesta.com). Check for the Bits and Jiggles night on Mondays at **Siberia** (2227 St Claude, 504 265 8855, www.siberianola.com) – you'll see some of the edgier dancers do sets between comedians. Finally, newish tiki bar Tiki Tolteca (301 North Peters, 504 267 4406) has dancers on Thursday evenings from around 8pm to midnight.

Honourable mention: A new club, Lucky Pierre's (735 Bourbon Street, 504 785 7441), has burlesque Thursdays-Sundays with some of the city's best talent, on show at just $5.

11. FREE LAUGHS

New Orleans hasn't traditionally been a comedy city, especially when compared to, say, New York or Chicago. Music really has been ruling the roost here for decades, if not centuries, and most bars will go with live music over live comedy to draw tourist crowds. However, a small group of dedicated local stand up comics have created a burgeoning scene, and you can now see good quality open mic nights for free almost every night of the week. These typically take place in bars (there are no comedy clubs as yet) across the city and if you're lucky, you'll even get to see nationally touring comedians who are passing through town. Drink minimums aren't real enforced, but these places are cheap in any case.

Monday

Siberia Comedy Night: A weekly free show in the Marigny from 9pm, sometimes with burlesque acts thrown in (Bits and Jiggles). 2227 St Claude, 504 265 8855, www.siberianola.com

Bear With Me: A weekly free show at Mid City favourite, neighbourhood bar 12 Mile Limit. Show starts at 8.30pm and they sometimes have free food as well. 500 S Telemachus Street, 504 488 8114

Gambit Comedy Night: Monthly free uptown show at 7pm. Publiq House, 4528 Freret Street, 504 826 9912

Tuesday

Comedy Beast: Weekly free show at 8pm. Howlin' Wolf Den, 907 South Peters, 504 529 5844, www.thehowlinwolf.com

Give 'Em the Light: Weekly free show in the French Quarter from 8pm. House of Blues, 225 Decatur Street, 504 301 4999, www.houseofblues.com

Comedy Catastrophe: Weekly free show from 10pm. Lost Love Lounge, 2529 Dauphine Street, 504 949 2009, www.lostlovelounge.com

Wednesday

Think You're Funny: Weekly free show from 9pm. Carrollton Station, 8140 Willow Street, 504 865 9190, www.carrolltonstation.com

Thursday

Comedy Gumbeaux: Weekly free show from 8.30pm. Howlin' Wolf Den, 907 South Peters, 504 529 5844, www.thehowlinwolf.com

All-Star Comedy Revue: Weekly free show from 8pm. House of Blues, 225 Decatur Street, 504 301 4999, www.houseofblues.com

Friday

The Upper Quarter: Weekly free show from 11pm. The Upper Quarter, 1000 Bienville Street, 504 523 4111

Accessible Comedy: Free weekly show from midnight. Buffa's Bar and Lounge, 1001 Esplanade Avenue, 504 949 0038, www.buffasbar.com

Saturday

Local Uproar: Weekly free show from 7pm. AllWays Lounge, 2240 St Claude Ave, 504 218 5778, www.theallwayslounge.net

Sunday

NOLA Comedy Hour: A free weekly show from 8pm. HiHo Lounge, 2239 St Claude, 504 945 4446, www.hiholounge.net

Honourable mention:

The New Movement is a theatre that teaches courses in improvisational and sketch comedy, and has showcases of its graduating classes on a regular basis. These are typically just a few dollars and of a pretty good standard all in all. Check the website (www.newmovementtheater.com) for details of upcoming graduation shows.

12. FREE OUTDOORS

Of course, all of the outdoors is free, but there are a few special spots in New Orleans that are so attractive that it feels like you should have to pay for them, and these are the places we'll feature in this section.

"Take a day to Wank it up! Some of my favorite places are on the 'Best' Bank."

West Bank

The West Bank is where the sun rises in NOLA (obviously). Also known as The Best Bank, or simply the Wank (sorry, Brits), it's a short ferry ride (free at the time of writing though under review and could rise to $2) from the port off Canal Street. Take time to look back at the city as you cross – it's one of the best views of the downtown skyline. Once you're there, you can easily get to Old Algiers Main Street, which has churches, historic homes and Mardi Gras World, where floats for the annual festival are made and stored. There are a couple of small parks (try Confetti or Delcazal) and you can stop for a pint in a traditional English pub, The Crown and Anchor. All in all, a pretty ideal afternoon out and an easy escape from the heat and crowds of the French Quarter. (www.algierspoint.org).

Audubon Park

There's been a public park here since the turn of the 20th century, and it's named after the famous artist and naturalist (and serial bird shooter, if the legends are to be believed) John James Audubon. As well as the grand open green spaces, there's a 1.8 mile jogging path, picnic spots and shelters. Attractions within the park include the Audubon Trail Golf Course and the Audubon Zoo, parts of which you can glimpse through the trees on the outskirts. You can see some uncaged wildlife of the bird variety thanks to the species that flock to the Oschner Island Rookery, which attracts egrets and herons (www.auduboninstitute.com).

The Fly

Tucked behind Audubon Zoo across the Mississippi River levee, this is essentially just the waterfront portion of Audubon Park. However, it does have a special place in locals' hearts and is a truly great spot in its own right. You'll see all manner of New Orleanians here, just hanging out, tossing a Frisbee around, boiling some crawfish or making out as they watch the sun go down over the river. (Exposition Drive)

City Park

This park's opening in 1854 makes it one of the oldest urban parks in the country. It stretches across 1,300 acres and enchants visitors and locals with its historic oaks and moss canopies. In fact, the park contains the world's largest stand of mature live oaks, so that's quite something. It has a quaint, old fashioned carousel park, as well as more modern biking, jogging and walking paths. There are also (paid) tennis courts and a golf course. Free stuff to look at and wander around includes the Besthoff Sculpture Garden and the Botanical Gardens. Trust us, Spring and Fall are near-perfect times for a picnic here (www.neworleanscitypark.com).

Lake Pontchartrain

Head north through the suburbs of Metarie and you'll get to this huge body of water that sits overlooking the surrounding wetlands. There are some wonderful views to be had around the waterway, and a few activities that you can do for free. For instance, two sites along the lakeshore have the access for swimming: Pontchartrain Beach on the south shore and Fountainbleau State Park on the north shore. As the names of these spots suggest, there are beach areas here to relax in and watch the sailboats race along the waters (www.saveourlake.org).

The Jean Lafitte National Historical Park and Preserve

This is essentially six sites throughout southern Louisiana, and three of these are located in central New Orleans. **Chalmette Battlefield and National Cemetery** dates to 1815 and has the graves of Civil War veterans. In the French Quarter, the **Visitor Center** has interactive displays, murals, exhibits, and literature that details the history and culture of the city. For a more outdoorsy experience, the **Barataria Preserve** is a 20,000 acre park with picnic areas and hiking trails amid the bayous and swamps (www.nps.gov/jela).

Woldenberg Park

This charming redbrick promenade that crosses the 16-acres from Jackson Square to the Audubon Aquarium. It is part of the Audubon Institute and you can stop at park benches under shady magnolia and crepe myrtle trees to catch those impromptu second line parades.

The Audubon Aquarium of the Americas and Entergy IMAX Theatre are both adjacent to the park (www.auduboninstitute.com).

New Orleans Jazz Historical Park

This quirky park gives visitors a chance to learn about the all-pervasive musical history of New Orleans. You can pick up a walking tour map of the city, or attend one of the many free concerts and children's music workshops that are offered throughout the year. The park is open Tuesday through Saturday, from 9am to 5pm. (916 N. Peters Street, 504 589 4841, www.nps.gov/jazz).

Honourable mentions:

OK, so the streetcar fare is $1.25. But riding it uptown does mean that you get the best free tour of the Garden District, taking in some incredible houses and mansions, university campuses and the beauty of St Charles Avenue. When you get to the end of the line, you can take it right back to the Quarter, and it's perfect transportation no matter what the weather.

"Always try to have the right change for the streetcar."

13. FREE MISCELLANY

Here are some things that only loosely fitted into the categories above, so we'd like to finish with a mixed bag, and one that we think really shows off the eclectic, authentic nature of New Orleans. People try and tout Las Vegas as the place to escape and have fun, but it is just so downtrodden with rules and regulations. Spend any amount of time in NOLA and you'll soon see that wonderfully authentic adventures happen all the time, and can take you in unexpected directions. You just have to open yourself up to it. You won't regret it. Honest.

Alright, then. Some random free stuff:

Battle of New Orleans re-enactment. Crowds gather for services, talks and re-enactments by the Chalmette Battlefield unit of Jean Lafitte National Historical Park and Preserve. Over 150 living history experts in period dress bring the sights and sounds of January 8, 1815, to life (www.nps.gov/jela/battle-of-new-orleans-anniversary).

Take a photo with Fats Domino, Pete Fountain, or Al Hirt (OK, their statue equivalents) at Music Legends Park on Bourbon Street.

Leave your legacy at the Old Absinthe House. The bar was constructed in 1807 and for many years served the infamous green drink after from which it received its name. People have been leaving their business cards on the wall for years, and you can add yours.

Go on social bike ride: NOLA Social Ride is a friendly group of bike lovers that meet at least once a week to ride around, meet friends and stop off for the odd drink. The rides can be themed around interests (eg. music) or neighbourhoods and they're the nicest people you could wish to meet. Check out their website and the schedule for their famous 'Happy Thursday' rides. www.nolasocialride.org

Be awed by the Mercedes Benz Louisiana Superdome. NOLA's iconic stadium is home throughout the year to many major conventions and sporting events, including the Super Bowl, which will be held there in 2015. You can walk around (the outside) any time.

Take a dip at the W Hotel (333 Poydras Street, www.wneworleans.com). The hotel opens up its great swimming pool in August, so you can dive in and escape the heat.

Take in the horses and the hats. Heading to the race track on Thanksgiving is a tradition in New Orleans. It's the first day of the season, and the gates are open. Locals dress to the nines, so there's plenty of people watching to go along with the Sport of Kings. (www.fairgroundsracecourse.com).

Catch the holiday spirit. The festive season in the tropics is a little weird, but still atmospheric. There are Cathedral concerts, cooking demonstrations and much more going on during what the city calls 'Christmas New Orleans Style,' which runs the entire month of December (www.neworleanscvb.com/things-to-do/festivals/christmas-new-orleans-style).

Blast out a song. There are some lively free karaoke alternatives, including every night at Kajun's Pub (2256 St. Claude Avenue, 504 947 3735) and Fridays from 11pm at Lost Love Lounge (2529 Dauphine Street, 504 949 2009, www.lostlovelounge.com). Not for the feint-hearted: the Cat's Miaow (701 Bourbon Street, 504 523 2788, www.catskaraoke.com) is as raucous as it gets.

14. YOU ARE NOW FREE TO GO

Thanks for downloading/reading New Orleans For Free. All material is copyright Paul Oswell but it's pretty general so feel free to use it how you will. I run a small online travel magazine and you should check it out – it tries to do more than just create top ten lists and has great stories from around the world. Go to:

www.shandypockets.com

Thanks again, and enjoy New Orleans. I certainly do.

Made in the USA
San Bernardino, CA
03 December 2014